Manifesting My Pet Snake

Written by Avril Asson
Illustrated by Swapnil & Nirzhar

To request permission, contact the publisher at
CAANGroupLLC@gmail.com

Hardcover: ISBN 979-8-9870013-0-1
Paperback: ISBN 979-8-9870013-1-8
Ebook: ISBN 979-8-9870013-2-5

Library of Congress Number: 2022917699

Published by CAAN Group LLC

Hi, I'm Nyah, and I'm a creator. Yes, you read that right. I am a creator, and so are you! My mom and dad taught me that I can create and manifest things in my own life.

Manifesting is when you use your thoughts and feelings to make something happen. Mind-blowing, isn't it? But it's true, and I manifested something really special… a pet snake!

It all started when my mom and dad gave me a book about reptiles. I immediately fell in love with snakes. All types of snakes: corn snakes, pythons, black mambas… I couldn't get enough! I love their cute little faces and that they don't have any legs.

Reptiles
For KIDS
Reptiles For KIDS
COLOURING

I had to have one, so I asked my parents. Guess what they said? If you guessed NO WAY, you might be afraid of snakes just like they are. They said, "No way, Nyah, but we love that you know so much about snakes."

I was shut down. I went to bed that night feeling disappointed. I thought my parents were stopping my manifestation. I started to feel sad and even a bit mad. Then I remembered my parents saying "when you feel upset and can't change how you feel, just go to sleep". Sleeping it off helps me to have a fresh, positive start the next day.

Reptiles for KIDS
Reptiles for KIDS

The following day, I thought about how my parents always said, "Focus on what you want and not what you don't want." So, I continued learning about snakes, drawing snakes, and watching videos about snakes. My dad even took my brother, sister, and I to a reptile serpentarium. A serpentarium is a place where snakes are kept. My brother and sister were afraid of the poisonous snakes, but I was in awe.

When my 8th birthday came, I thought it was finally my chance to get a pet snake. There was no way they would say NO WAY on my birthday! So, I asked again, and guess what they said? If you answered yes, you must be a snake lover like me.

Unfortunately, they said, "Sure, Nyah, you can get a snake… when you move out and into your own house."

"What's another, less scary reptile that you like?" asked my mom. I thought long and hard and came up with a bearded dragon. My dad told me to make a list of all the reasons why I would want a bearded dragon. Can you guess what reason number 1 was?

Reason #1: I cannot have a snake until I am older.

Even though I liked bearded dragons, I was still focused on snakes. I felt happy when I read or looked at videos about them. I even imagined myself holding my future snake. I wasn't sad about my parents not getting me one. Instead, I felt joyful when I thought about my pet snake. I was also thankful that I might be getting a bearded dragon for my birthday.

We ♥ Snakes
2:00 / 10:00

On the day of my birthday party, my dad presented me with a big present covered with a blanket. I could tell it was a reptile terrarium, and I just knew it was a bearded dragon.

Nyah
Birthday Girl

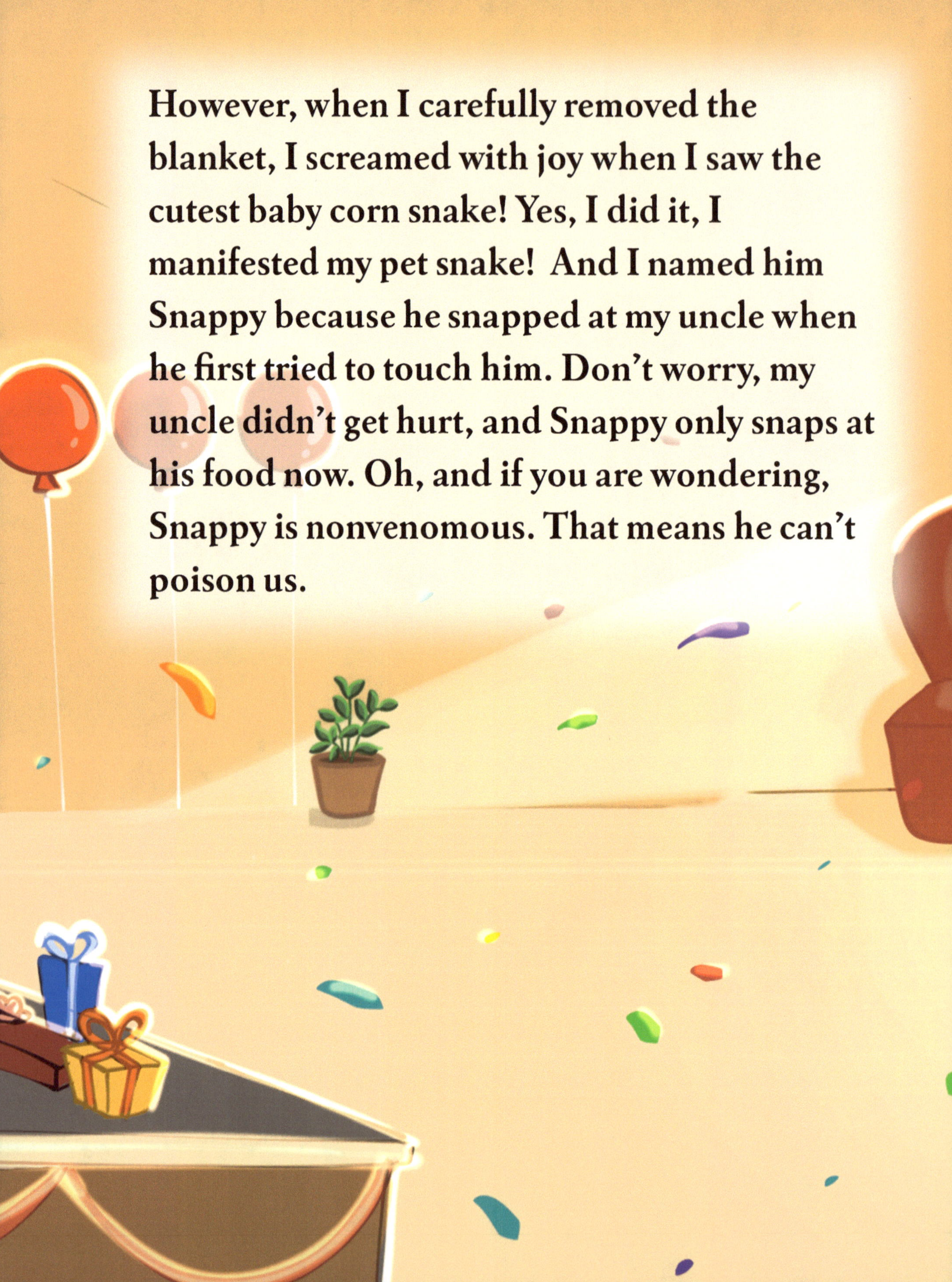

However, when I carefully removed the blanket, I screamed with joy when I saw the cutest baby corn snake! Yes, I did it, I manifested my pet snake! And I named him Snappy because he snapped at my uncle when he first tried to touch him. Don't worry, my uncle didn't get hurt, and Snappy only snaps at his food now. Oh, and if you are wondering, Snappy is nonvenomous. That means he can't poison us.

Can you believe it? My parents, who said there was NO WAY they would get me a snake, didn't stand in the way of my amazing creation and manifestation skills.

So how, or why, did my parents change their minds? Well, my parents went to the pet store to buy a bearded dragon. The pet store attendant helped them pick one out, along with the tank and decorations for it. But when it came time to buy the food for the bearded dragon, my parents said NO WAY to buying live crickets.

Reptile food
Bug Box
Bug Box
Bug Box
Live Cricket
Live Cricket
Live Cricket
Live Cricket

My mom said she was disgusted when she looked at the crickets. My dad said they were loud and smelly. The thought of having dozens of live crickets in our house made my parents say **NO WAY** to the bearded dragon.

My uncle, who happened to be at the pet store with my parents joked, "I guess now Nyah has to get a pet snake". See, the bearded dragon ate lots of live crickets a few times a week, while the snake only ate two small, frozen mice once a week. So, my parents chose the snake instead. Live crickets and frozen mice are both gross to me, but I'm happy to say I feed Snappy two frozen mice every Wednesday.

Creating and manifesting can be easy, we all do it every day. Here are a few tips to help you out:

1. Think about what you want, not what you don't want. Although my parents first said NO WAY to a pet snake, I continued to read, draw and watch videos about snakes.

2. Practice gratitude and find happiness in the little things. A bearded dragon was my second choice, but I was still thankful to be getting one as a pet.

3. Use your imagination and your mind to see what you want. I would imagine myself holding my future snake almost every day, feeding it and watching its skin shed.

4. If you feel negative emotions and it is hard to change the way you feel, try going to sleep and starting over when you wake up. The day after my parents told me NO WAY, I continued to love and learn more about snakes.

Now that you know how to manifest, join me in learning to become amazing creators of our lives. Can't wait to see what you manifest!

Acknowledgments

I have to start by thanking my amazing husband, Chris. Thank you for your support throughout this whole literary process. Above all, thank you, Chris, for leading our family to a better awareness of who we truly are. To my daughter, Nyah, thank you for applying this knowledge of self and becoming the inspiration for this book. To my family and friends, thank you for the time spent listening to me, supporting me, and for your vital advice. To Snappy, thank you for being you. Thank you to my editors for taking the time to send your detailed comments and feedback. This book is better thanks to you all.

About the Author

Avril Asson was born in the beautiful island of Trinidad and Tobago. She is now settled in Florida with her husband and four lovely children. Avril defines herself as a devoted family person. Her dedication is seen through her zeal to homeschool her children and instill positive thinking and manifesting skills. She has a vision to empower children across the globe to practice skills to be intentional creators of the life that they want.